CONTENTS

Preface
Step 1 - Select your hardware   1
Step 2 - Hardware Setup   4
Step 3 - Setup Network   10
Step 4 - Connect Remotely   13
Step 5 - install binaries   17
Mid-way Checkpoint   19
Step 6 - Bitcoin wallet   21
Step 7 - Mining Pool   24
Step 8 - Configure Miner   27
Step 9 - Moment of truth   30
Step 10 - Buy a yacht   33

PREFACE

Bitcoin is a technological tour de force. - Bill Gates

Bitcoin is the beginning of something great: a currency without a government, something necessary and imperative. For beginner bitcoin enthusiasts mining for BTC can be overwhelming. If you fall into this category, this book is for you. This guide outlines, in nuanced detail the exact steps one needs to take to create a bitcoin mining rig, including hardware and software. This book will show you how to go from 0 to 100 by providing detailed step by step instructions on how to set up a bitcoin mining rig for under $99. We will reference only official documentation. After reading this book, you will have a fully functioning mining rig connected to a mining pool with a bitcoin wallet, mining for BTC while you sleep. You will know how to calculate profit and loss. You will know the characteristics of a machine that makes money, and the characteristics of a machine that loses money. Your machine will be profitable in the current economic climate.

This book will guide you past all of the issues glossed over on the the popular bitcoin forums while also showing you how much you can expect to make (or lose) with this mining configuration and others. This book will provide you with a head-first dive into the world of bitcoin mining. In the spirit of transparency, here's all the software and hardware you'll need for this book. In each chapter we will break it down line by line.

List of components needed to mine bitcoin

#	Component	Type	Cost
1	Raspberry Pi v3 or higher	Hardware	$35
2	Gekkoscience 2pac USB BM1384x2 or higher	Hardware	$30
3	SanDisk Pro MicroSD 64GB+ Adapter	Hardware	$28
4	Raspbian Stretch	Software	$0
5	SD Formatter 4.0	Software	$0
6	Win32Disk Imager	Software	$0
7	Putty	Software	$0
8	Advsanced IP Scanner	Software	$0
9	Edge bitcoin wallet	Software	$0
10	Slushpool	Software	$0
11	Cgminer	Software	$0

Enjoy the journey.

STEP 1 - SELECT YOUR HARDWARE

Bitcoin is exciting because it shows how cheap it can be. Bitcoin is better than currency in that you don't have to be physically in the same place and, of course, for large transactions, currency can get pretty inconvenient." - John McAfee

Here is the expected hardware investment. You will need to purchase two devices as part of step 1. All of this can be purchased on Amazon.

Component	Price
Raspberry Pi v3 or higher	$35
Gekkoscience 2pac USB BM1384 x2 or higher	$30
Sandisk Pro MicoSD 64GB+	$20
Total	**$85**

Step 1a: Buy a machine — Raspberry Pi 3 or higher — Cost : $30USD

This is a bare-bones machine powered by a distro of linux called Raspbian. Don't buy the upgraded versions w/ premium casing or an upgraded power supply. The $35 will work. Get it on the cheap, you're here to learn. Retail on amazon is approximately $30USD.

Step 1b: Buy an ASIC USB mining stick to connect to the Raspberry Pi 3 — Gekkoscience 2pac USB — Cost : $35USD

The raspberry pi 3 is not going to mine the bitcoin for you. It is the device which is used to connect to the actual 'mining rig', in this case, a USB bitcoin stickminer from Gekkoscience.

The technical documentation indicates up to 15 Gh/s but the Raspberry Pi 3 doesn't have enough voltage 'out of the box' to run it at full capacity without an external power supply. We are doing this on the cheap and as a result you can realistically expect somewhere around 7Gh/s. In fact, the max G/hs I was able to achieve was > of 9Gh/s within the slushpool mining pool:

Block ID	Block Found At	Duration	Pool Scoring Hash Rate	Your Scoring Hash Rate	Your Reward	Block Value	Confirmations Left
38142	2018-12-25 11:31	01:49:33	3.888 th/s	78.99 Mh/s	0.00000000 btc	12.62427412 btc	91
38141	2018-12-25 09:42	02:56:04	3.901 th/s	7.175 gh/s	0.00000002 btc	12.59788897 btc	79
38140	2018-12-25 06:46	00:32:32	3.909 th/s	---	0.00000000 btc	12.98270604 btc	61
38139	2018-12-25 06:13	00:50:51	3.878 th/s	---	0.00000000 btc	12.58503421 btc	59
38138	2018-12-25 05:22	02:58:47	3.881 th/s	---	0.00000000 btc	13.28714012 btc	53
38137	2018-12-25 02:24	01:44:49	3.821 th/s	9.058 Mh/s	0.00000000 btc	12.83148439 btc	42
38136	2018-12-25 00:39	00:31:54	3.860 th/s	1.710 gh/s	0.00000001 btc	12.62749440 btc	29
38135	2018-12-25 00:07	01:14:36	3.849 th/s	5.054 gh/s	0.00000002 btc	12.57171270 btc	24
38134	2018-12-24 22:52	00:51:21	3.842 th/s	4.402 gh/s	0.00000002 btc	12.50000000 btc	15
38133	2018-12-24 22:01	00:27:57	3.871 th/s	8.465 gh/s	0.00000003 btc	12.70356732 btc	5
38132	2018-12-24 21:33	03:23:55	3.878 th/s	3.317 gh/s	0.00000001 btc	12.58849267 btc	1
38131	2018-12-24 18:09	00:30:04	3.875 th/s	1.749 gh/s	0.00000001 btc	12.53881723 btc	Confirmed
38130	2018-12-24 17:39	05:14:58	3.877 th/s	7.863 gh/s	0.00000003 btc	12.53535392 btc	Confirmed
38129	2018-12-24 12:24	01:28:55	3.901 th/s	---	0.00000000 btc	12.58505051 btc	Confirmed
38128	2018-12-24 10:55	01:03:46	3.902 th/s	---	0.00000000 btc	12.77449742 btc	Confirmed

Step 1c: Buy a microSD card + adapter — SanDisk 64GB — Cost: $28USD

The raspberry pi 3 doesn't actually come with any disk space, but it has a MicroSD port which can be used to install the Raspberry PI OS (Raspbian), mining pool binaries (cgminer) and distro updates. **64gb is plenty.**

STEP 2 - HARDWARE SETUP

"We have elected to put our money and faith in a mathematical framework that is free of politics and human error." – Tyler Winklevoss

By now you now have the cheapest raspberry pi 3 you can find, a gekkoscience 2pac usb miner BM1384, and a 64gb microSD card + adapter. Now we need to download the Raspberry Pi Raspbian OS, format the SD card, install the raspberry Pi OS onto the SD card, and enable SSH tunneling. Here is the software you'll need to download, don't worry, it's free. By the end of step 2, you will be able to remotely connect to your raspberry Pi.

Software	Price
Raspbian Stretch with Desktop and Recommended Software	$0
SD Formatter 4.0	$0
Win32Disk Imager	$0
Total	$0

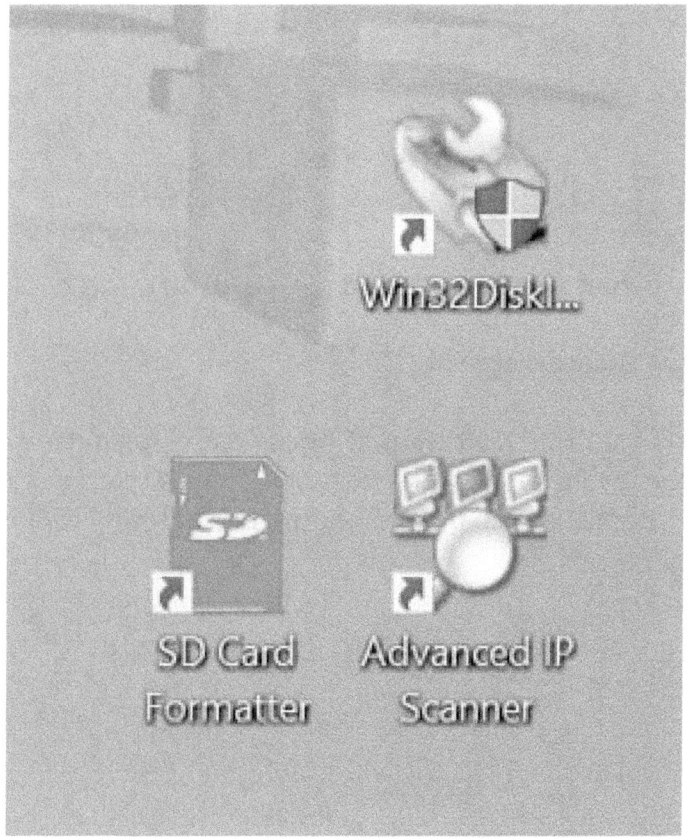

Step 2a: Download the Raspbian Stretch with Desktop and recommended software

URL: www.raspberrypi.org

This contains the single image (.img) for the Raspbian OS. Download the zipped version and unzip to directory of your choice, in my example I unzipped it to C:\rasp

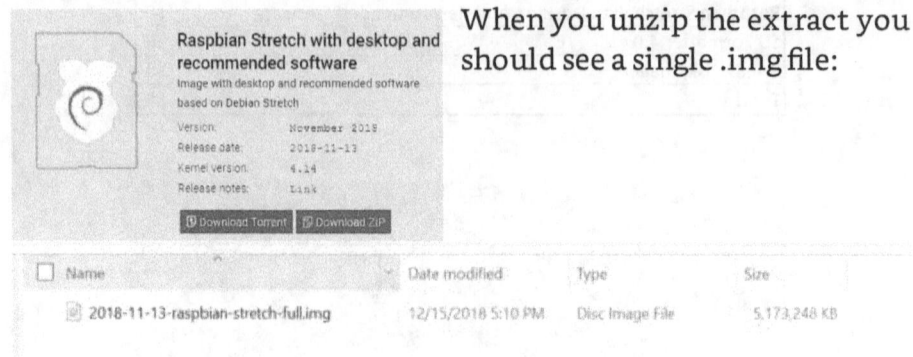

When you unzip the extract you should see a single .img file:

Step 2b: Format the SD card using SD Card Formatter

URL: www.sdcard.org

The blank microSD you bought needs to be formatted prior to having the raspbian img installed. My MicroSD card automaps to drive D, which I used to format as outlined below. This is a 3 click process.

STEP 2 - HARDWARE SETUP

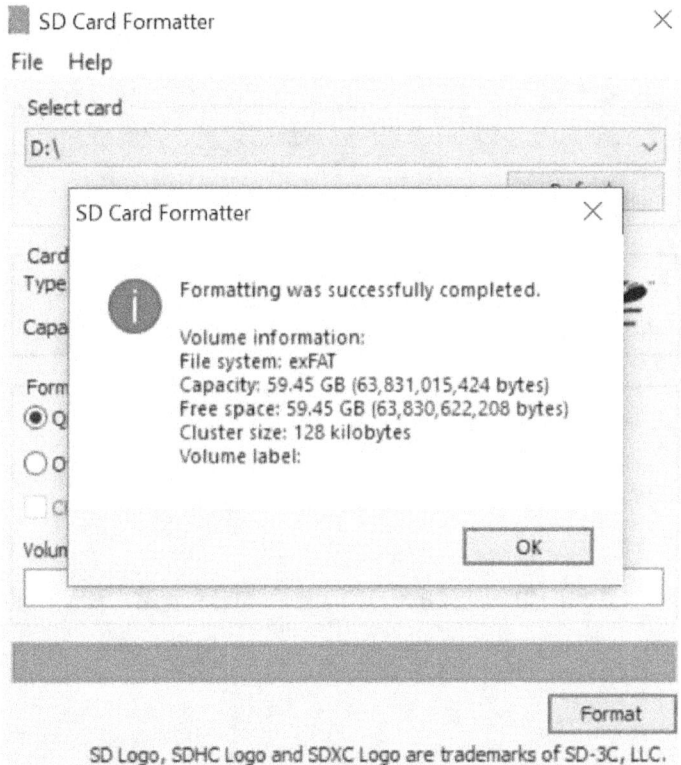

Step 2c: Install the Raspberry Pi Raspbian OS using Win32Disk Imager

URL: https://sourceforge.net/projects/win32diskimager/

Use Win32Disk Imager will decompress the .img file and install the Raspbian binaries to the microSD card.

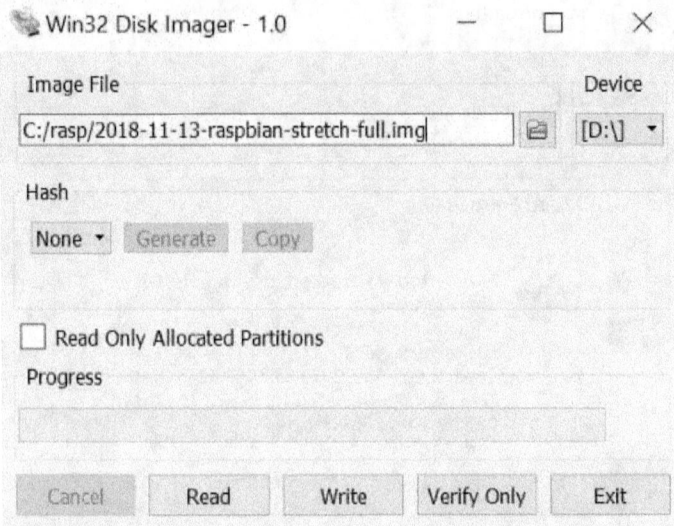

If you open the microSD card, you will see the following:

Step 2d: Enable ssh on the Raspberry Pi OS

So i'm not connecting a monitor directly to the raspberry pi because it doesn't have enough voltage to support my HDMI display and I'm sure as hell not going to buy a new monitor for this experiment. As a result, i'm going to connect to raspberry pi via via a remote terminal called 'putty', this is also called 'headless'.

start.elf	11/12/2018 5:25 PM	ELF File	2,791 KB
start_cd.elf	11/12/2018 5:25 PM	ELF File	663 KB
start_db.elf	11/12/2018 5:25 PM	ELF File	5,001 KB
start_x.elf	11/12/2018 5:25 PM	ELF File	3,963 KB
ssh	12/25/2018 1:43 PM	File	0 KB

To enable ssh, create a file called 'ssh' (without '), no extension, into the root directory of the microSD card. When the raspberry Pi boots up, ssh will become enabled, and the file will be deleted.

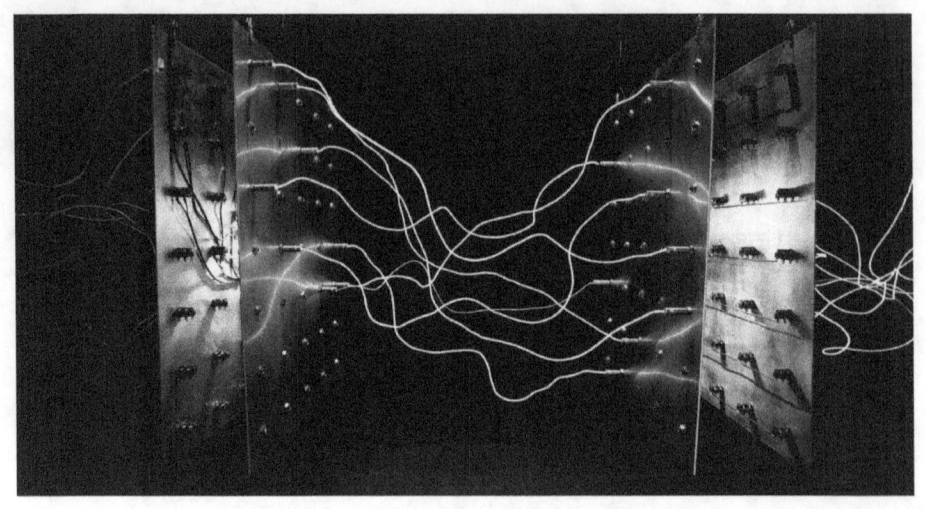

STEP 3 - SETUP NETWORK

"Bitcoin may be the TCP/IP of money." – Paul Buchheit

This is the first time we'll actually power on the mining rig. Keep in mind it needs to be located somewhere close to your modem or router. You should have the:

1. The MicroSD card embedded into the Raspberry Pi micro SD port.

2. The Gekko USB stick connected to one of the 4 raspberry pi USB ports.

3. The Raspberry Pi connected to your network via a cat 5 cable.

4. The Raspberry Pi should be powered on.

This is the result: The fan should be on, Raspberry Pi & Gekko-science USB stick should be green.

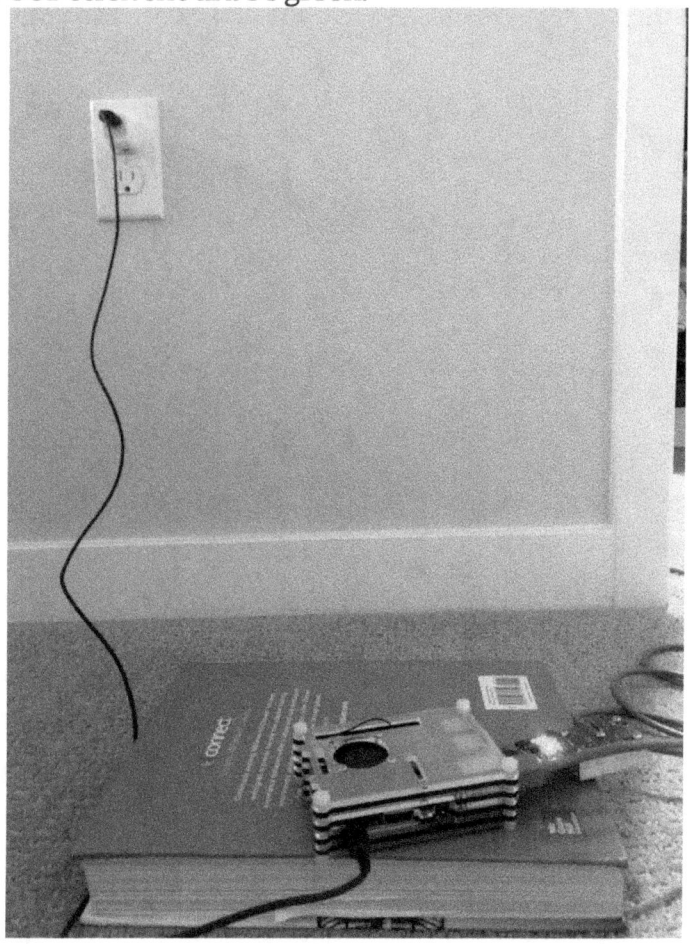

Here's a pic of the cat 5 cable running to the router:

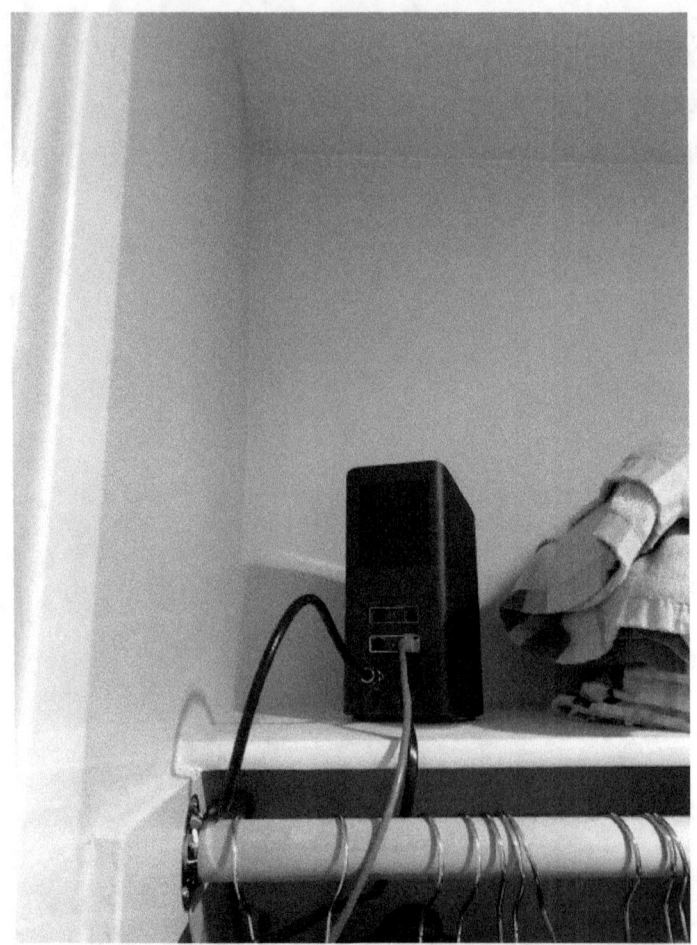

STEP 4 - CONNECT REMOTELY

"Bitcoin, and the ideas behind it, will be a disrupter to the traditional notions of currency. In the end, currency will be better for it." – Edmund C. Moy

Now you have a Raspberry Pi powered on somewhere in your house, maybe your closet? But your physical computer is somewhere else, how do we connect to the raspberry Pi? The answer is command line via putty. In this step we will need to download 2 applications:

Software Title	Price
Putty	$0
Advanced IP Scanner	$0
Total	$0

Step 4a: Find the Raspberry Pi 3 IP Address with Advanced IP scanner

URL: www.advanced-ip-scanner.com

The raspberry pi is sitting somewhere on your network, and you need to know your IP address in order to ssh into it. Using Advanced IP Scanner on my network i'm able to find the machine under IP address 10.0.0.191. You can see I have other devices on my network, IP/mac addresses have been redacted.

Step 4b: Connect to the Raspberry Pi via putty

URL: www.putty.org

When we open putty, let's be sure to connect to the IP address associated with the Raspberry Pi device which we found in our previous step, in this example — 10.0.0.191:

STEP 4 - CONNECT REMOTELY

Once you hit open, connect with root account:

Username = pi
password = raspberry

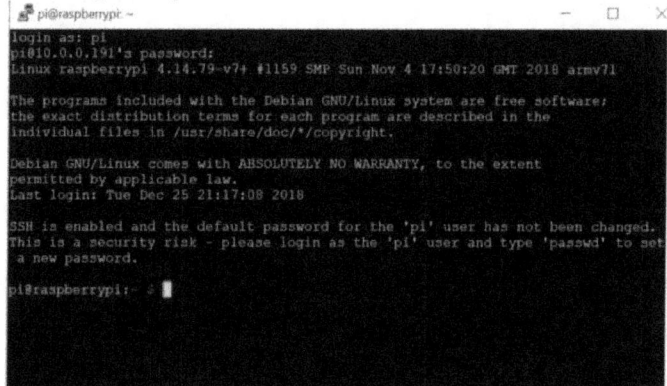

Do you feel like like the hacker from the 80s classic movie **War**

Games? Because I definitely did.

STEP 5 - INSTALL BINARIES

"Bitcoin is here to stay". - Adam Draper

This was probably one of the most difficult steps because there are a series of required binaries which need to be installed prior to connecting to the miningpool via cgminer. The existing documentation doesn't cover the pre-requisites files, and if you don't install all of the required binaries you will get error messages like:

"AM_PATH_LIBGCRYPT missing; CLI tool will not be available" when launching cgminer.

Step 5a: Run the following command lines via putty:

1. sudo apt-get update;

2. sudo apt-get install git-core -y;

3. sudo apt-get install autoconf autogen libtool uthash-dev libjansson-dev libcurl4-openssl-dev libusb-dev libncurses5-dev;

4. sudo apt-get install libevent-dev;

5. sudo apt-get install libusb-1.0;

6. sudo apt-get install build-essential pkg-config libjansson-dev uthash-dev libncursesw5-dev libudev-dev libmicrohttpd-dev libhidapi-dev;

You can try to run these in one big apt-get install command but I found peace with myself by running each command in smaller breakout statements.

All of the apt-get install commands should produce a series of steps similar to the screen above which culminate with a successful 'done'.

MID-WAY CHECKPOINT

"Bitcoin will do to banks what email did to the postal industry". - Rick Falkvinge

We are half way through this odyssey. Let's recap what we've accomplished thus far:

Step 1 - Hardware acquisition: We've bought the cheapest possible mining rig possible: A raspberry pi, Gekkoscience USB mining stick, and micro SD card. Out of pocket total should be less than $99.

Step 2 - Software set up: With the required hardware in our possession, we then downloaded Raspbian stretch, formatted our micro SD card and installed the stretch using win32 disk imager.

Step 3 - Initial power-on & Network connectivity: We then powered on the raspberry pi using stretch while ensuring it was connected to our network via a cat5 cable.

Step 4 - Remote connectivity: With the mining rig on and connected to our network our next step is to remote into the rig from another machine. To achieve this we used Advanced IP scanner to identify the rig IP address. With the IP address identified with ssh'ed into the machine via putty.

Step 5 - Binary update: By now we are ssh'ed into to the rig which is on our internet-enabled network. We proceed to install all required binaries needed to join a mining pool. To achieve this we used Advanced package tool (apt-get) to install git-core and all required packages.

We have now completed all pre-requisites and we're ready to to mine. Next we'll:

Step 6 - Create a bitcoin wallet.

Step 7 - Join a mining pool.

Step 8 - Add our mining rig to the mining pool

Step 9 - Start mining

Step 10 - Buy a yacht (maybe)

STEP 6 - BITCOIN WALLET

"There is a big industry around bitcoin. People have made fortunates offf Bitcoin. it is volatile, but people make money off of volatility too". - Richard Branson

When you successfully mine bitcoin, the mining pool would need pay you that bitcoin (less their mining fees). To do this they would transfer the currency to your wallet. There's a ton wallet options available at **bitcoin.org** . In this guide we're going to use the Edge bitcoin wallet because it's easily accessible via your iPhone and the wallet provisioning process takes only a few clicks.

Software Title	Price
Edge	$0
Total	$0

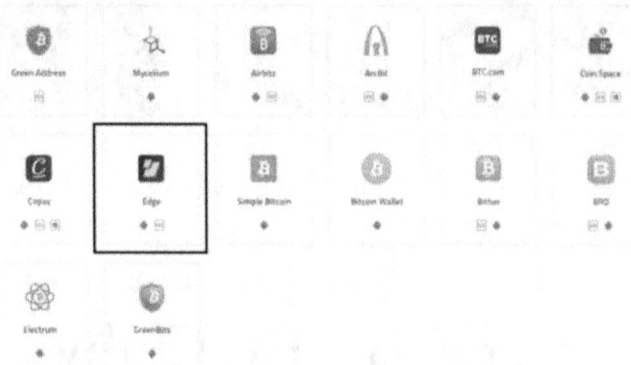

Once you have your account set up, you'll be provided with a bitcoin receiving wallet address like mine below:

STEP 6 - BITCOIN WALLET   23

Note if you have an existing bitcoin wallet through coinbase, etc, feel free to use that in place of edge.

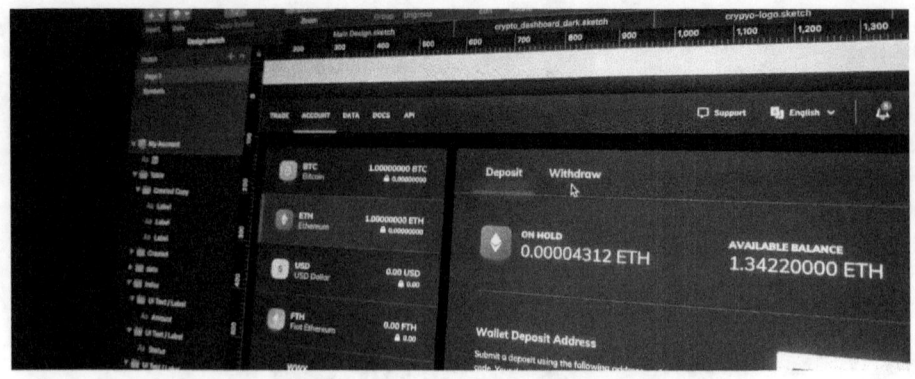

STEP 7 - MINING POOL

"The crypto market will reach $80 trillion within 15 years." - Tim Draper

Imagine you want to mine gold, in real life. You have 2 options:

Option 1: Go mine gold on your own with your own resources.

Option 2: Join a large group which is already mining gold, and share in the gold which is found. Bitcoin is no different, we're going to join a mining pool and allocate the resources (Giga-hashes) from our machine into the pool at large. In exchange, we'll share in the pool's profits and pay the pool operator a small fee of 2%.

In this step, we are joining a mining pool called slushpool.

STEP 7 - MINING POOL

Software Title	Price
Slushpool.com	$0
Total	**$0**

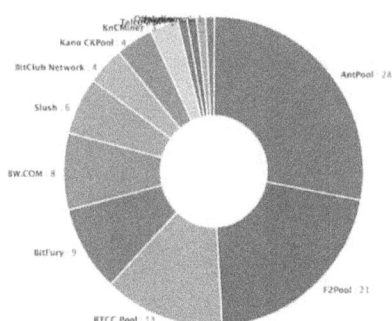

As of the time of this writing, there were 13 major bitcoin mining pool operators. I've chosen Slushpool since it was the first mining pool created, and has an easy to use GUI.

Step 7a: Make a slushpool account and add your bitcoin receiving wallet

URL: https://slushpool.com

When you register an account a slushpool you can navigate to Settings -> Bitcoin -> Payouts and add the bitcoin receiving wallet address created in step 6 to your slushpool profile.

Step 7b: Save your Slushpool Server Address

When you register an account a slushpool you can navigate to Settings -> Bitcoin -> Payouts and add the bitcoin receiving wallet address created in step 6 to your slushpool profile.

Under Help Center -> Getting Started Bitcoin you will find the slushpool server addresses currently available. We are going to use US east. Use this server closest to you. Take note and save it

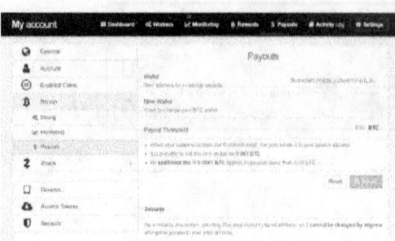

for step 9.

Servers Location	Address
USA, east coast	stratum+tcp://us-east.stratum.slushpool.com:3333
Canada	stratum+tcp://ca.stratum.slushpool.com:3333
Europe	stratum+tcp://eu.stratum.slushpool.com:3333
Singapore, South Asia	stratum+tcp://sg.stratum.slushpool.com:3333
Japan, Pacific	stratum+tcp://jp.stratum.slushpool.com:3333
China, mainland	stratum+tcp://cn.stratum.slushpool.com:3333 stratum+tcp://cn.stratum.slushpool.com:443 stratum+tcp://cn02.stratum.slushpool.com:3333 stratum+tcp://cn02.stratum.slushpool.com:443 stratum+tcp://cn03.stratum.slushpool.com:3333 stratum+tcp://cn03.stratum.slushpool.com:443

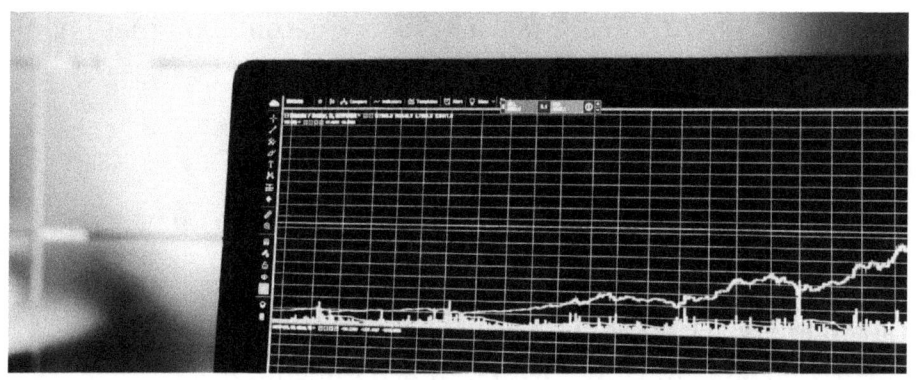

STEP 8 - CONFIGURE MINER

"Bitcoin, and the ideas behind it, will be a disrupter to the traditional notions of currency". - Edmund Moy

We need to download and install the software that will actually perform the mining. So far we have the hardware (gekko USB stick) and a mining pool account (slushpool). We are going to install cgminer on our raspberry pi, which will use the gekko USB stick to mine bitcoins within the slushpool mining pool.

I originally spun my wheels for nearly a week trying to get BFGminer working on the raspberry pi only to find out (as of this writing) there isn't a clear path to configure the Gekkoscience USB

2pac BM1384 with BFGMiner. This was a painful less that I hope you can avoid. See the official threads:

1 - Gekkoscience Support Thread URL:

https://bitcointalk.org/index.php?topic=1764803.0

2 - Github gekkoscience Support for BFGMiner URL:

https://github.com/luke-jr/bfgminer/issues/692

For this reason, and 3 micro SD card formats later, we're going to use CGminer.

Software Title	Price
cgminer	$0
Total	**$0**

Step 8a: Download & configure cgminer

URL: https://github.com/vthoang/cgminer

We need to download a forked version of cgminer which was built specificlly for the Gekkoscience 2pac USB BM1384 devices. Here is the official support thread, you should bookmark this as I spent hours combing through the 106 page thread. URL: https://bitcointalk.org/index.php?topic=1764803.0

Within putty terminal, run:

1. mkdir -p git/vthoang; cd git/vthoang;
git clone https://github.com/vthoang/cgminer.git;
cd cgminer;

This will download the fork of the Gekkosicence 2pac USB cg-

STEP 8 - CONFIGURE MINER

miner codebase located at github.com/vthoang

Now run the configuration shell script for cgminer and recompile the folder using the command 'make'

2. CFLAGS="-O2 -march=native" ./autogen.sh — enable-gekko; make -j 2;

Grant cgminer access to the gekkoscience 2pac usb miner by running:

3. cd ~/git/vthoang/cgminer/
sudo usermod -G plugdev -a `whoami`
sudo cp 01-cgminer.rules /etc/udev/rules.d/
sudo reboot

If you don't do this, when you run cgminer you will get a "USB init, open device failed" ... "you don't have privilege to access" error. Note that this command will also reboot your Raspberry Pi 3.

STEP 9 - MOMENT OF TRUTH

It is common sense to take a method and try it. If it fails, admit it frankly and try another. But above all, try something." - Franklin Roosevelt

Getting to this step took a better part of a week, with a bunch of trial and errors. My big hurdles were understanding the compatibility problems with BFGminer and the power limitations of the gekko USB stick. Let's start mining bitcoin

To run cgminer , enter the following command via putty to your raspberry pi:

1. ./cgminer -o stratum+tcp://us-east.stratum.s-

STEP 9 - MOMENT OF TRUTH

lushpool.com:3333 -u **yourslushpoolaccount.slushpoolworkername** -p x — suggest-diff 32 — gekko-2pac-freq 100

Replace "yourslushpoolacount.slushpoolworkername" with the information created in step 7a.

What do you see? Failure? I noticed that whenever I ran cgminer at BM1384's default speed of 100mhz, the USB device would enter disabled or zombie mode, which means that no mining is taking place.

When we review the official Gekkoscience 2pac usb BM1384 support thread: https://bitcointalk.org/index.php?topic=1764803.0

We see that in post 10 of page 1, a warning to all raspberry PI users:

> *They have trouble even supplying enough current to a portable USB self-powered HDD... let alone a stickminer =) I don't want to see people with unnecessary troubles related to this =)*

Unfortunately I didn't see that warning..for atleast 6 hours. A tough lesson that I hope you can avoid. Since we're doing this **on the cheap** and and want to spend **as little money as possible** , instead of going out and buying a powered hub, we're going to reduce the frequency of the stickminer from 100mhz to 50mhz. Run the following command in putty. Note how we're telling cgminer to reduce the mining speed to 50mhz.

1. ./cgminer -o stratum+tcp://us-east.stratum.slushpool.com:3333 -u yourslushpoolaccount.slushpoolworkername -p x — suggest-diff 32 — gekko-2pac-freq **50**

If the stars are aligned and you click your heels together 3 times, the cgminer installed on your raspberry pi 3 will join the slushpool us east mining pool and mine bitcoin with the gekkoscience 2pac usb 1384 mining stick:

```
cgminer version 4.11.1 - Started: [2018-12-25 00:18:28.988]
--------------------------------------------------------------
 (5s):2.102G (1m):849.4M (5m):204.5M (15m):70.41M (avg):2.926Gh/s
 A:0  R:8192  HW:0  WU:40.1/m
 Connected to us-east.stratum.slushpool.com diff 8.19K with stratum as user
 Block: 11d763d2...  Diff:5.11T  Started: [00:18:31.171] Best share: 41
--------------------------------------------------------------
 [U]SB management [P]ool management [S]ettings [D]isplay options [Q]uit
 0: GSD 10022344: BM1384:2 50.00MHz       | 2.132G / 2.870Gh/s WU:40.1/m
--------------------------------------------------------------
 [2018-12-25 00:18:27.683] Started cgminer 4.11.1
 [2018-12-25 00:18:27.684] Probing for an alive pool
 [2018-12-25 00:18:27.887] Pool 0 difficulty changed to 8192
 [2018-12-25 00:18:28.072] Rejected untracked stratum share from pool 0
 [2018-12-25 00:18:28.931] GSD 0: 2Pac BM1384 Bitcoin Miner (10022344)
 [2018-12-25 00:18:28.990] Network diff set to 5.11T
 [2018-12-25 00:18:29.194] GSD 0: found 2 chip(s)
 [2018-12-25 00:18:29.253] GSD 0: setting frequency to 50.00MHz
 [2018-12-25 00:18:29.260] GSD 0: open cores @ 50.00MHz
 [2018-12-25 00:18:29.900] GSD 0: start work @ 50.00MHz
 [2018-12-25 00:18:31.172] Stratum from pool 0 detected new block at height 555334
```

STEP 10 - BUY A YACHT

"Right now bitcoin feels like the internet before the browser" - Wences Casares

Just kidding..step 10 doesn't involve a yacht party, bottles and models, or telling your boss to pound sand. Now that we're mining bitcoin, let's answer the only question that really matters: **Am I making any MONEY?**

By logging into my slushpool.com payout screen and I can my machine's contribution to the overall mining pool, as well as my reward. In this experiment I let this mining rig run from Christmas day 1200am to 200pm. What is the result? Did we create wealth?

Reward History

Visit User Manual for more information about how your rewards are calculated. ⧉ User Manual

Block ID	Block Found At	Duration	Pool Scoring Hash Rate	Your Scoring Hash Rate	Your Reward	Block Value	Confirmations Left
38145	2018-12-25 16:04	00:38:07	3.940 Eh/s	214.4 Mh/s	0.00000000 BTC	12.57373547 BTC	99
38144	2018-12-25 15:26	02:24:11	3.863 Eh/s	1.442 Gh/s	0.00000001 BTC	12.50838065 BTC	96
38143	2018-12-25 13:02	01:30:36	3.886 Eh/s	1.057 Gh/s	0.00000000 BTC	12.58703268 BTC	74
38142	2018-12-25 11:31	01:49:33	3.888 Eh/s	78.99 Mh/s	0.00000000 BTC	12.62427412 BTC	64
38141	2018-12-25 09:42	02:56:04	3.901 Eh/s	7.175 Gh/s	0.00000002 BTC	12.59786697 BTC	52
38140	2018-12-25 06:46	00:32:32	3.909 Eh/s	---	0.00000000 BTC	12.86270604 BTC	34
38139	2018-12-25 06:13	00:50:51	3.878 Eh/s	---	0.00000000 BTC	12.58503421 BTC	32
38138	2018-12-25 05:22	02:58:47	3.881 Eh/s	---	0.00000000 BTC	13.28714012 BTC	26
38137	2018-12-25 02:24	01:44:49	3.821 Eh/s	9.058 Mh/s	0.00000000 BTC	12.83148439 BTC	15
38136	2018-12-25 00:39	00:31:54	3.860 Eh/s	1.710 Gh/s	0.00000001 BTC	12.62749440 BTC	2

Taking block ID 38141 as an example, the pool's aggregate hash rate was 3.901 E/hs which mined a block value worth 12.59788697 bitcoin. My contribution was a hash rate of 7.17G/hs for which I was paid 0.00000002 bitcoin. Let's do some math (1 BTC = $3769.99USD). Replace this number with the current price of BTC.

Total Bitcoin mined & dollar value Christmas Day 2018

Block	Block Found At	Duration	Pool Scoring	Your Scoring	Your Reward (B	Block Value (BT	Your Reward Value	Total Block Value
38145	12/25/2018 16:04	0:38:07	3.940 Eh/s	214.4 Mh/s	0.000000000	12.573735470	$ -	$ 47,402.856984545
38144	12/25/2018 15:26	2:24:11	3.863 Eh/s	1.442 Gh/s	0.000000010	12.508380650	$ 0.000037700	$ 47,156.469966694
38143	12/25/2018 13:02	1:30:36	3.886 Eh/s	1.057 Gh/s	0.000000000	12.587032680	$ -	$ 47,452.987333273
38142	12/25/2018 11:31	1:49:33	3.888 Eh/s	78.99 Mh/s	0.000000000	12.624274120	$ -	$ 47,593.387189659
38141	12/25/2018 9:42	2:56:04	3.901 Eh/s	7.175 Gh/s	0.000000020	12.597866970	$ 0.000075400	$ 47,493.832498230
38140	12/25/2018 6:46	0:32:32	3.909 Eh/s	---	0.000000000	12.862706040	$ -	$ 48,492.273143740
38139	12/25/2018 6:13	0:50:51	3.878 Eh/s	---	0.000000000	12.585034210	$ -	$ 47,445.453121358
38138	12/25/2018 5:22	2:58:47	3.881 Eh/s	---	0.000000000	13.287140120	$ -	$ 50,092.385380999
38137	12/25/2018 2:24	1:44:49	3.821 Eh/s	9.058 Mh/s	0.000000000	12.831484390	$ -	$ 48,374.567835456
38136	12/25/2018 0:39	0:31:54	3.860 Eh/s	1.710 Gh/s	0.000000010	12.627494400	$ 0.000037700	$ 47,605.527613056
38135	12/25/2018 0:07	1:14:36	3.849 Eh/s	5.054 Gh/s	0.000000020	12.571712700	$ 0.000075400	$ 47,395.231161873
38134	12/24/2018 22:52	0:51:21	3.842 Eh/s	4.402 Gh/s	0.000000020	12.500000000	$ 0.000075400	$ 47,124.875000000
38133	12/24/2018 22:01	0:27:57	3.871 Eh/s	8.465 Gh/s	0.000000030	12.703567320	$ 0.000113100	$ 47,892.321760727
38132	12/24/2018 21:33	3:23:55	3.878 Eh/s	3.317 Gh/s	0.000000010	12.588492670	$ 0.000037700	$ 47,458.491480973
38131	12/24/2018 18:09	0:30:04	3.875 Eh/s	1.749 Gh/s	0.000000010	12.538817230	$ 0.000037700	$ 47,271.215568928
				Total:	0.00000013	189.98773897	$ 0.000490099	$716,251.876039510

Source: www.medium.com/educatedandbroke

The pool's total block value over the 12 to 16 hour window was approximately $716.251USD, my baby $99 mining rig's payout? $0.0004 cents. That's less than one one-hundredth of one penny.

Also take into consideration that each mining pool as minimum payout thresholds. For slushpool i've set it at 0.01 bitcoin:

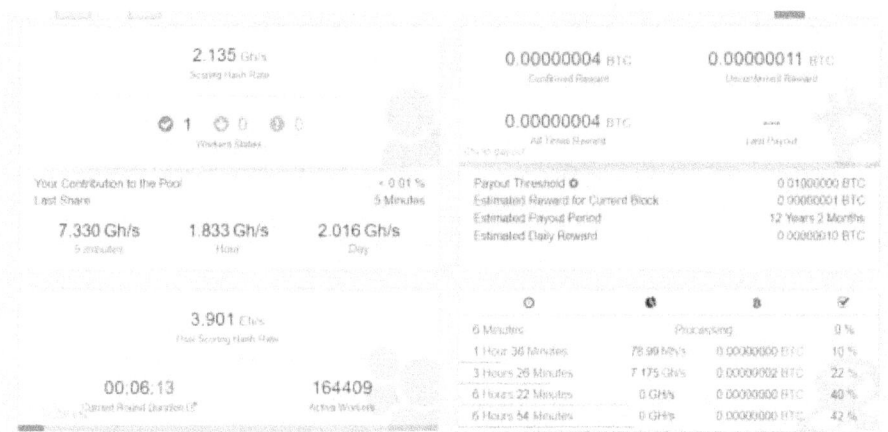

With the machine's hash rate of 7G/hs combined w/ the current mining complexity, i will hit the minimum payout of .01 BTC in **12 years.**

How long it will take to meet minimum payout

1 BTC (USD)	$	3,769.99
Minimum Payout (BTC)		0.01
Minimum Payout Value	$	37.70
Years to meet payout minimum		12
Earnings per year	$	3.14

Source: www.medium.com/educatedandbroke

What about electricity?

Remember that this machine, no matter how cheap, costs *you* money to operate, this is electricity. Gekkoscience's technical documentation indicates this device will use approximately 7.5watts of power to operate per hour. If we look at the the **United States' Electricity profile** we can see that the average cost of 1 kilowatt in the state of California is 15.23 cents. We can use that to calculate annual operating costs for our mining rig:

Mining rig power calculation	
Power (watts)	7.50
Power (kWh)	0.01
Hours On	24
Days On	365
Price kWh	$0.12000
Cost per day	$0.02160
Cost per month	$0.65700
Cost per year	**$7.88000**

When we put the operating costs and anticipated profitability together, we see that our payback period when bitcoin is priced at $3800 is NEVER. The machine is not proftiable, it operates at a loss every year. For this rig to be protiftable, the price of 1 BTC would need to be atleast $9,000.

Profit/Loss for Mining Rig			
Year	Earnings	Cost	Profit
1	$ 3.14	$ 7.88	$ (4.74)
2	$ 3.14	$ 7.88	$ (4.74)
3	$ 3.14	$ 7.88	$ (4.74)
4	$ 3.14	$ 7.88	$ (4.74)
5	$ 3.14	$ 7.88	$ (4.74)
6	$ 3.14	$ 7.88	$ (4.74)
7	$ 3.14	$ 7.88	$ (4.74)
8	$ 3.14	$ 7.88	$ (4.74)
9	$ 3.14	$ 7.88	$ (4.74)
10	$ 3.14	$ 7.88	$ (4.74)
11	$ 3.14	$ 7.88	$ (4.74)
12	$ 3.14	$ 7.88	$ (4.74)
Total:	$ 37.68	$ 94.56	$ (56.88)

Not only have you learned how to mine bitcoin, but more importantly, you've learned how to mine bitcoin profitability. If you take this information, acquire a powerful mining rig with low electricity costs, you are now in a position to mine bitcoin and create wealth. Enjoy.

www.ingramcontent.com/pod-product-compliance
Lightning Source LLC
Chambersburg PA
CBHW050306220526
45465CB00002B/844